Best Easy Day Hikes
Tacoma

Help Us Keep This Guide Up to Date

Every effort has been made by the author and editors to make this guide as accurate and useful as possible. However, many things can change after a guide is published—trails are rerouted, regulations change, facilities come under new management, etc.

We would love to hear from you concerning your experiences with this guide and how you feel it could be improved and kept up to date. While we may not be able to respond to all comments and suggestions, we'll take them to heart and we'll also make certain to share them with the author. Please send your comments and suggestions to the following address:

Globe Pequot Press
Reader Response/Editorial Department
P.O. Box 480
Guilford, CT 06437

Or you may e-mail us at:

editorial@GlobePequot.com

Thanks for your input, and happy trails!

Best Easy Day Hikes Series

Best Easy Day Hikes
Tacoma

Allen Cox

GUILFORD, CONNECTICUT
HELENA, MONTANA

AN IMPRINT OF GLOBE PEQUOT PRESS

FALCONGUIDES®

Copyright © 2010 by Morris Book Publishing, LLC

FalconGuides is an imprint of Globe Pequot Press.

Falcon, FalconGuides, and Outfit Your Mind are registered trademarks
of Morris Book Publishing, LLC.

Maps by Off Route, Inc. © Morris Book Publishing, LLC
Project editor: John Burbidge
Layout artist: Kevin Mak

Library of Congress Cataloging-in-Publication Data
Cox, Allen.
  Best easy day hikes, Tacoma / Allen Cox.
      p. cm.
  ISBN 978-0-7627-5457-1
  1. Hiking—Washington (State)—Tacoma Region—Guidebooks. 2.
Tacoma Region (Wash.)—Guidebooks. I. Title.
  GV199.42.W22T334 2010
  917.797'788–dc22

                                              2010001410

Printed in the United States of America
10 9 8 7 6 5 4 3 2 1

Contents

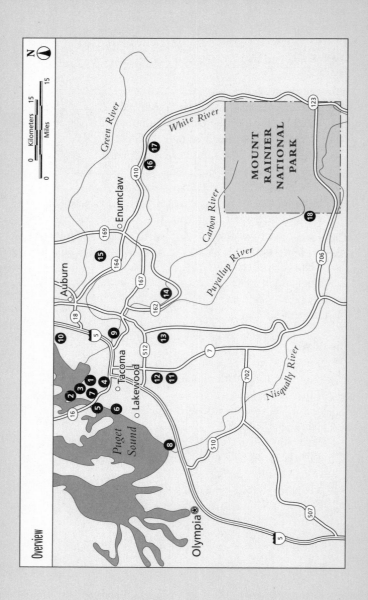

Overview

MOUNT RAINIER NATIONAL PARK

Acknowledgments

First I would like to extend my appreciation to all who advocate for sensible land management and the conservation of public lands and wild habitats. Without their work, few places such as the ones included in this guidebook would be set aside for the rest of us to enjoy.

I would like to thank the land management agencies responsible for the trails included in this guidebook for their cooperation and assistance: Metro Parks Tacoma, City of Federal Way, Pierce County Parks and Recreation, Pierce County Chambers Creek Properties, Washington State Department of Transportation, Washington State Parks, US Fish and Wildlife Service, US Forest Service, and the US Army Corps of Engineers.

My sincere appreciation goes out to my editor, Scott Adams, and the outstanding team at Globe Pequot Press for their guidance and clarity in helping me shape this guide-book.

Lastly, I am grateful to Robert Pruett, Roger Ward, and Dana Price, my dear friends and hiking companions, who know how to appreciate an easy day hike better than anyone. Without them, researching this book would have required many lonely hours on the trail.

Introduction

The Landscape from Sound to Summit

With 42 miles of Puget Sound shoreline within the Tacoma city limits and foothills rising to mountain peaks beyond, the Tacoma area encompasses widely diverse types of terrain. A large part of the city sits on a peninsula extending into south Puget Sound. At the tip of the peninsula, a vast urban forest has been preserved as one of the city's environmental and recreational treasures. Outside the city, wildlife refuges, river and farm valleys, small towns and suburbs, and wooded hills make up the greater Tacoma area, with the second highest peak in the Lower 48 a near and awesome presence about an hour's drive to the southeast.

What does this landscape do for recreational opportunities in and around the city? If you guessed boating, sailing, swimming, scuba diving, bicycling, jogging, climbing, skiing, and even parasailing, you'd be correct. But let's not forget about hiking.

Many who call this area home love to hit the trail and take out-of-towners along on the walk. Networks of trails in and around the city offer a variety of settings and terrains, from urban waterfront hikes with stunning views of the sound and islands to quiet treks through remote wilderness areas to rails-to-trails routes built on retired railroad beds linking many of the area's towns.

With this kind of variety, there's a trail in the Tacoma area to suit every ability, and all have one thing in common: a close-up view of nature. This guidebook has attempted to select the Tacoma area's best easy day hikes.

Tacoma-Area Boundaries and Corridors

For the purposes of this guide, the best easy day hikes are located in Tacoma, Pierce County, northern Thurston County, and southern King County. Each hike is confined to no more than a 75-minute drive from downtown Tacoma under normal traffic conditions.

I-5 is the principal north-south artery in western Washington; Tacoma is situated roughly halfway between Seattle and Olympia on this interstate. Highways 7, 706, 512, and 410 are the main routes connecting Tacoma to the Cascades and Mt. Rainier. Highway 16 heads west across Puget Sound to the Kitsap Peninsula via the Narrows Bridge; however, none of the hikes in this book are located across Puget Sound or on any of the islands west of Tacoma. Driving directions to the trailheads are provided from either downtown Tacoma or from I-5.

Weather

With four distinct seasons, few extremes, and an average of fifty-eight days of clear, sunny days per year, Tacoma generally enjoys a cool, temperate climate. Like Seattle, the city has earned a reputation as a soggy spot, but actually only receives about 39 inches of annual rainfall.

Tacoma is situated in the Puget Sound Basin between the Olympic and Cascade Ranges with 14,410-foot Mt. Rainier only an hour away. Clouds move in from the Pacific and can remain for long stretches. When it rains, the Tacoma area tends to get soaked with protracted periods of drizzle. The rainiest seasons are late fall and winter, when strong Pacific storms occasionally blow through.

There's no denying that when the sun comes out in

western Washington it's cause for rejoicing, but the region's cloudy, damp days possess their own beauty too. The forests glisten and come alive. Fog and mist shroud the hilltops and define contours otherwise not seen. The air is fresh, with grit and dust washed away. With the right gear, you can enjoy the local trails whatever the weather.

Part of being prepared for your hike is checking the weather forecast. If weather conditions are potentially hazardous, which is rare, postpone your hike. If weather conditions are favorable to a safe experience on the trail, enjoy yourself, rain or shine.

Wildlife

Marine wildlife, birds, and woodland animals share the spotlight with scenery on trails in and around Tacoma. From deer, bald eagles, and an occasional red fox in Point Defiance Park to goldeneyes performing mating rituals in Commencement Bay, it's hard to take a hike in the area without observing wildlife. The Tacoma Nature Center, operated by Metro Parks Tacoma, and the US Fish and Wildlife Service's Nisqually National Wildlife Refuge are hubs of wildlife education in the region, and this guidebook includes trails at both locations.

Of course it's possible to take a hike in and around Tacoma without seeing anything more than a few seagulls combing the beach. Wildlife doesn't usually stage an entrance just to be noticed by humans. Be on the lookout for the wild inhabitants near the trail and you might be surprised at what critters are watching *you*.

Encounters with large wildlife are extremely rare but not unheard of, especially as our habitat encroaches on theirs.

Some trailheads post information about what to do if you encounter a bear or cougar. An excellent source of information regarding such encounters is "Living with Wildlife," available on the Washington Department of Fish and Wildlife Web site at www.wdfw.wa.gov/wlm/living/.

Be Prepared

Hiking in Tacoma and the surrounding area is generally safe. Still, you should be prepared, whether you are out for an urban hike along Tacoma's waterfront or venturing into the Cascades. The following tips will help you get ready for your hike:

- Research trail conditions in advance by checking the appropriate land management agency's Web site or calling their office.
- Check the weather forecast. If it predicts potentially hazardous weather, postpone your hike.
- Hazards along some trails include uneven footing, steep drop-offs, and slippery trail surfaces, such as mud, ice, and wet boardwalks. Trekking poles and proper footwear with good tread can help you maintain your balance in more challenging areas.
- Carry a large enough backpack for the essentials and any extras you might want, such as guidebooks, cameras, and binoculars. The essentials you should carry on every hike are a map, compass, water and water filtration method, food, rain gear and extra clothing, matches and fire starter, first-aid kit, army knife or multipurpose tool, flashlight and extra bulbs, sunscreen, and sunglasses. These essentials are especially important on nonurban hikes.

- Know the basics of first aid, including how to treat bleeding, bites, stings, fractures, strains, sprains, and contact with poison oak and stinging nettles. Pack a first-aid kit, no matter how short your excursion.

- While heat stroke and heat exhaustion are unlikely in Tacoma's climate, hiking on hot summer days brings risks. Heat exhaustion symptoms include heavy sweating, muscle cramps, headache, dizziness, and fainting. Should you or your companions exhibit any of these symptoms, cool the victim down immediately by rehydrating and getting him or her to an air-conditioned location. Cold showers also help reduce body temperature. Heat stroke is much more serious: The victim may lose consciousness, and the skin is hot and dry to the touch. In this event, call 911 immediately.

- Prepare for extremes of both heat and cold by dressing in layers.

- Regardless of the weather, your body needs water while hiking. A full thirty-two-ounce bottle is the recommended minimum for these short hikes, but more is always better. Bring a full water bottle, whether water is available along the trail or not.

- Don't drink from streams, rivers, creeks, or lakes without first treating or filtering the water. Water from such sources may host a variety of contaminants, including giardia, which can cause serious intestinal unrest.

- Most area trails have cell phone coverage. Bring your device, but make sure you turn it off or put it on the vibrate setting if you are hiking in a place where a cell phone ring might disturb wildlife or fellow hikers.

- Make sure children don't stray from the designated route. Children should carry a whistle; if they become lost, they should stay in one place and blow the whistle to summon help.

- Many of the waterfront hikes in this book border areas that are not safe for swimming. Swim at designated swimming beaches only, with a companion and preferably a lifeguard present.

Zero Impact

Trails in the Tacoma area are heavily used year-round. We, as trail users and advocates, must be especially vigilant to make sure our passage leaves no lasting mark. Here are some basic guidelines for preserving trails:

- Pack out all your own trash, including biodegradable items like orange peels, or deposit it in a designated trash container. You might also pack out garbage left by less considerate hikers.

- Don't approach or feed wildlife—the squirrel eyeing your energy bar is best able to survive if it remains self-reliant.

- Don't pick wildflowers or gather rocks or other treasures along the trail. Removing these items will only take away from the next hiker's experience.

- Stay on the established route to avoid damaging trailside soils and plants. This is also a good rule of thumb for avoiding poison oak and stinging nettle, common regional trailside irritants.

- Don't create shortcuts, which can promote erosion and damage native vegetation.

- Be courteous by not making loud noises while hiking.

- Many of these trails are multiuse, which means you'll share them with other hikers, runners, skaters, bicyclists, and equestrians. Familiarize yourself with the proper trail etiquette. As a pedestrian, you generally have the right-of-way, but you should yield when common sense dictates.

- Use restrooms and outhouses at trailheads or along the trail.

Land Management

The following government and private organizations manage the public lands described in this guide and can provide maps and information on these and other trails in their service areas:

- Metro Parks Tacoma, 4702 S. 19th St., Tacoma 98405; (253) 305-1000, TTY (253) 759-9286; www.metroparkstacoma.org.

- City of Federal Way Parks, Recreation and Cultural Services, P.O. Box 9718, Federal Way 98063-9718; (253) 835-6901; www.cityoffederalway.com.

- Pierce County Parks and Recreation, 9112 Lakewood Dr. SW, Lakewood 98499; (253) 798-4176; www.co.pierce.wa.us.

- Pierce County Chambers Creek Properties, 9850 64th Street West, University Place 98467; call Pierce County Parks and Recreation (253) 798-4176; www.piercecountywa.org/pc/abtus/ourorg/ccp/index.htm.

- Thurston County Parks and Recreation, 4131 Mud Bay Rd. SW, Olympia 98502; (360) 786-5595, TDD (360) 754-2933; www.co.thurston.wa.us/parks.

- Washington State Department of Transportation, P.O. Box 47300, Olympia 98504-7300; (360) 705-7000; www.wsdot.wa.gov.

- Washington State Parks, 1111 Israel Rd. SW, Tumwater 98504-2650; (360) 902-8844; www.parks.wa.gov.

- US Fish and Wildlife Service, Nisqually National Wildlife Refuge, 100 Brown Farm Rd., Olympia 98516; (360) 753-9467; www.fws.gov/Nisqually.

- US Forest Service, Gifford Pinchot National Forest, 11024 US 12, Randle 98377; (360) 891-5000, TTY: (360) 487-1100; www.fs.fed.us/gpnf.

- US Army Corps of Engineers, 30525 SE Mud Mountain Rd., Enumclaw 98022-8010; (360) 825-8211; www.nws.usace.army.mil/PublicMenu/Menu.cfm?sitename=MM&pagename=Tour.

Public Transportation

This guidebook includes driving directions to trailheads but does not include information on public transportation routes, schedules, or fares. Pierce Transit and Sound Transit serve the Tacoma area. For Pierce Transit, call (253) 581-8000, or visit www.piercetransit.org. For Sound Transit, call (206) 398-5000 or (800) 201-4900, or visit www.soundtransit.org.

How to Use This Guide

This guide is designed to be simple and easy to use. Each hike is described with a map and summary information that delivers the trail's vital statistics, including length, difficulty, fees and permits, park hours, canine compatibility, and trail contacts. Directions to the trailhead are also provided with trailhead GPS coordinates, along with a general description of what you'll see along the way. A detailed route finder (Miles and Directions) provides mileages between significant landmarks along the trail.

Hike Selection

This guide describes trails that are accessible to every hiker. The longest route is 5 miles round-trip, although many can be extended with connecting trails. They range in difficulty level from flat excursions perfect for a family outing to more challenging hikes with some elevation gain. These trails were selected to represent a wide diversity of terrain, scenery, and experiences. Keep in mind that nearby trails, often in the same park or preserve, may offer options better suited to your needs and abilities. These hikes are spaced throughout the Tacoma area—wherever your starting point, you'll find a great easy day hike nearby.

Difficulty Ratings

These are all easy hikes, but easy is a relative term. In the Tacoma area, hills are a fact of life, but many of the hikes in this guide have no elevation gain at all; others have moderate elevation gain.

To aid in the selection of a hike that suits your particular needs and abilities, each hike is rated easy, moderate, or more challenging. Bear in mind that even challenging routes can be made easier by hiking within your limits, being prepared, using trekking poles, and resting when you need to.

- **Easy** hikes are generally short and flat, taking no longer than an hour or two to complete.
- **Moderate** hikes involve increased distance and/or slight changes in elevation or may take longer than one to two hours to complete.
- **More challenging** hikes feature some steep stretches, more elevation gain, greater distances, more difficult terrain, or may take longer than two hours to complete.

These ratings are subjective. What you consider easy is entirely dependent on your level of fitness and the adequacy of your gear (primarily shoes). If you are hiking with a group, you should select a hike with a rating that's appropriate for the least fit and least prepared hiker in your party.

Approximate hiking times are based on the assumption that on flat ground, most walkers average 2.5 miles per hour. Adjust that rate by the steepness of the terrain and your level of fitness (subtract time if you're an aerobic animal; add time if you're hiking with kids or are easily distracted by trailside attractions), and you will arrive at an approximate hiking duration. Be sure to add more time if you plan to take part in other activities, such as picnicking, bird-watching, or photography.

Trail Finder

Map Legend

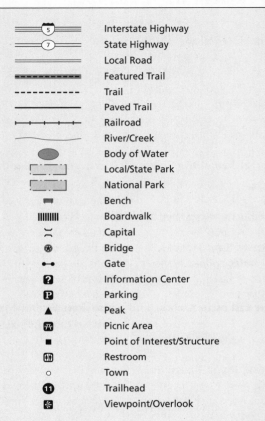

═══⑤═══	Interstate Highway
───⑦───	State Highway
═══════	Local Road
▬▬▬▬▬▬▬	Featured Trail
- - - - - - -	Trail
━━━━━━━	Paved Trail
⊢⊢⊢⊢⊢⊢⊢	Railroad
∼∼∼∼∼∼	River/Creek
⬭	Body of Water
▭▭	Local/State Park
▭▭	National Park
═	Bench
‖‖‖‖‖‖	Boardwalk
⏝	Capital
✪	Bridge
•–•	Gate
❷	Information Center
🅿	Parking
▲	Peak
⊼	Picnic Area
■	Point of Interest/Structure
🚻	Restroom
○	Town
⓫	Trailhead
⚐	Viewpoint/Overlook

1 Ruston Way Waterfront

This waterfront promenade is a magnet for Tacoma residents and visitors year-round, and with one visit it's easy to see why. The views of the Olympic and Cascade ranges, Puget Sound, Commencement Bay, Vashon Island, and 14,410-foot Mt. Rainier make this one of Tacoma's most scenic areas. The promenade links several parks, public piers, restaurants, and a few relics from Tacoma's past, and ends at Old Town, where the city's pioneers settled.

Distance: 4.2 miles out and back

Approximate hiking time: 2 hours

Difficulty: Easy, flat trail

Trail surface: Paved, a short section of gravel

Best season: Year-round

Other trail users: Skaters, bicycles

Canine compatibility: Leashed dogs permitted

Fees and permits: No fees or permits required

Schedule: Ruston Way is open 24 hours a day every day; the parks are open dawn to dusk.

Maps: USGS Tacoma North, WA; Tacoma street map

Trail contacts: Metro Parks Tacoma; (253) 305-1000; www .metroparkstacoma.org

Finding the trailhead: From downtown Tacoma, drive north on Pacific Avenue, which becomes Schuster Parkway. Take the North Ruston Way exit off Schuster Parkway, and follow North Ruston Way along the waterfront, past Marine Park, and to a narrow parking lot on the right between Ruston Way and the water. Turn right into the parking lot. GPS: N47 17.56' / W122 29.71'

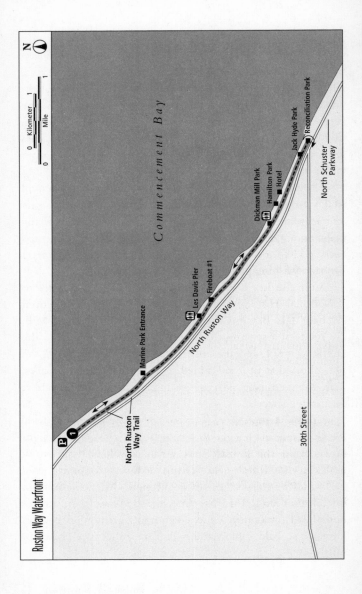

Ruston Way Waterfront

Commencement Bay

North Ruston Way Trail

Marine Park Entrance

Les Davis Pier

Fireboat #1

North Ruston Way

Dickman Mill Park

Hamilton Park

Hotel

Jack Hyde Park

Reconciliation Park

North Schuster Parkway

30th Street

N

0   Kilometer   1

0   Mile   1

The Hike

In Tacoma's infancy, Ruston Way—then Front Street, where boatyards, sawmills, warehouses, and other enterprises once lined the waterfront—was the centerpiece of the city's commercial life. Today, few relics of Tacoma's industrial past remain. Instead, parks, public piers, six waterfront restaurants, and a hotel occupy this scenic shoreline with a long promenade connecting it all.

Begin the hike at the north end of the promenade and walk southeast (toward the port). The first park you'll come to is Marine Park, an extensive stretch with lawns, picnic tables and benches, a pedestrian pier, a beach that's a popular entry point for scuba divers, and the Les Davis Pier, a long T-shaped fishing pier.

After the Les Davis Pier, the promenade continues to a National Historic Landmark dating from 1929: retired Fireboat #1. Beyond that are the ruins of Dickman Mill, the relics of a sawmill that continuously operated from the 1890s to 1974. It later burned, and the city acquired the site, cleaned it up, and added it to its collection of parks. The only remnants are pilings, today an important habitat for marine species.

Hiking Ruston Way is a rewarding experience anytime but is a special treat at low tide, when the view straight down from the public piers yields a colorful garden of undersea life from giant starfish attached to pilings and bulkheads to colonies of sea anemones. Other wildlife not uncommon along this shoreline include waterfowl, such as bufflehead, goldeneye, and cormorant, great blue herons, kingfishers, bald eagles, and seals that sometimes glide just off shore.

Next, you will come to Hamilton Park, a shady lawn with tables and benches at the water's edge and a U-shaped public pier that surrounds a waterfront hotel. Farther along, Old Town Dock, constructed in 1873, still stands but is closed in the interest of public safety. Across Ruston Way from the dock and 1 block uphill is Old Town, Tacoma's first neighborhood, now a historic district that's worth a detour.

After Old Town Dock, continue a short distance along Ruston Way. The trail ends at Jack Hyde Park and a new park under construction as of the writing of this guidebook, Reconciliation Park, designed to mark a dark chapter in Tacoma's history: the tragic expulsion of Chinese immigrants from the city in 1885. There, you will turn around and retrace your steps back to the starting point.

Miles and Directions

- **0.0** From the parking lot, walk southeast along Ruston Way.
- **0.4** Marine Park begins.
- **0.9** Pass Les Davis Fishing Pier, snack bar, bait shop, and restrooms.
- **1.0** Pass Fireboat #1.
- **1.5** Dickman Mill Park begins.
- **1.6** Pass Dickman Mill ruins, viewpoint pier, beach, and restrooms.
- **1.7** Pass Hamilton Park; turn left onto the U-shaped pier that circles the hotel.
- **1.9** Turn left and continue along Ruston Way.
- **2.0** Pass Old Town Dock.
- **2.1** Enter Jack Hyde Park; loop to the left at Reconciliation Park (under construction) and retrace your steps.
- **4.2** Arrive back at the starting point.

2 Point Defiance Park: Spine–Outer Loop–Inner Loop Trails

Tacoma's more than one-hundred-year-old Point Defiance Park not only houses a renowned zoo and aquarium, extensive gardens, a logging museum, and a living history museum at Fort Nisqually but also hundreds of acres of urban forest laced with trails. The three main trail routes are marked with geometric symbols: the Spine Trail is a circle, the Outer Loop Trail a square, and the Inner Loop a triangle. The route prescribed here takes in segments of all three trails.

Distance: 3.7-mile double loop

Approximate hiking time: 2 hours

Difficulty: Moderate due to a few inclines, and often muddy conditions

Trail surface: Gravel, dirt

Best season: Year-round

Other trail users: None

Canine compatibility: Leashed

dogs permitted

Fees and permits: No fees or permits required

Schedule: Sunrise to sunset every day

Maps: USGS Gig Harbor, WA; Tacoma street map

Trail contacts: Metro Parks Tacoma; (253) 305-1000; www.metroparkstacoma.org

Finding the trailhead: From I-5, take exit 132 onto WA 16. Take exit 3 (Sixth Avenue) off WA 16, and at the second stoplight turn right onto North Pearl Street. Stay on North Pearl Street (WA 163), which will end at Point Defiance Park. Drive into the park and follow the signs to Five Mile Drive. Park in the Rustic Picnic Area parking lot or along the road at the Rhododendron Garden. GPS: N47 18.55' / W122 31.48'

The Hike

At more than 700 acres, the wooded peninsula known as Point Defiance is home to one of the greatest remaining forests in North America inside an urban core.

This popular park's trail system is a major recreational hub for hikers and runners. The trail surface consists of gravel near the trailhead, but soon it becomes a dirt surface, and segments can be extremely muddy and slippery for days after a rain. Good treads and trekking poles can help you navigate the muddy trail surface.

With three main trails and numerous trail combinations, hikers in Point Defiance have many choices. A park map that includes trails is posted on a kiosk along the main road shortly after the park's main entrance, just before the Japanese Garden. It's easy for those unfamiliar with the park's trail system to become disoriented without paying attention to the trail markers; a map and a GPS receiver can be very handy for staying on course. Of course, if you follow the circle, square, or triangle trail symbols, you will complete your hike easily. Following a route that's a combination of the three trails, such as the one described here, adds a bit more challenge—and fun.

The park's forest is a classic temperate rain forest environment with a high canopy of ancient cedars, Douglas firs, hemlocks, and maples providing shade for layers of verdant, emerald undergrowth, featuring many species of mosses and ferns.

The Spine Trail (circle symbol) traces the center of the peninsula through old-growth forest all the way to the point that is the park's namesake. The Outer Loop Trail (square symbol) begins on the Spine Trail but soon branches off

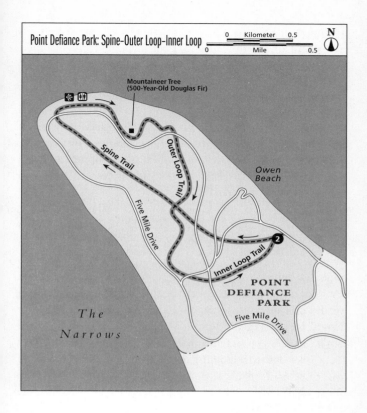

Point Defiance Park: Spine-Outer Loop-Inner Loop

Kilometer

Mile

N

Mountaineer Tree
(500-Year-Old Douglas Fir)

Spine Trail

Outer Loop Trail

Five Mile Drive

Owen
Beach

Inner Loop Trail

2

POINT
DEFIANCE
PARK

Five Mile Drive

The
Narrows

and follows the outer perimeter of the peninsula atop 100-foot bluffs with excellent views of Puget Sound, islands, and mountains. The Inner Loop Trail (triangle symbol) also begins on the Spine Trail but soon traces its own circular route through the deep forest. The route prescribed here follows the Spine Trail for its entire length, then joins the Outer Loop Trail along a segment that takes in the views and passes the Mountaineer Tree (a more than 500-year-old

Douglas fir), detours onto a connector trail, and finally joins a segment of the Inner Loop Trail through a quiet section of old-growth.

Whether you stick to one of the three routes or follow a combination of trails, Point Defiance provides an enriching forest experience right in the city.

Miles and Directions

0.0 The trail begins at the RHODODENDRON GARDEN sign. Follow the trail uphill a short distance to the picnic shelter and turn right at the trail marker with the circle symbol (Spine Trail).

0.2 Come to a Y and turn right (follow the circle symbol).

0.3 Come to a trail crossroads; continue straight ahead, and in a short distance cross two roads, one immediately after the other, and continue on the trail (follow the circle symbol).

0.5 Cross the road and continue on the trail (follow the circle symbol). On the Spine Trail, you will pass through several trail intersections, but continue straight ahead (follow the circle symbols).

1.4 Come to a picnic shelter with a view of the water; turn right onto the Outer Loop Trail (follow the square symbol), which follows the road a short distance and then enters the woods on the left.

1.6 The trail crosses a viewpoint parking lot and enters the woods again (follow the square symbol).

1.8 Come to the Mountaineer Tree (a Douglas fir more than 500 years old), and continue on the trail (follow the square symbol).

2.3 Cross a viewpoint parking lot and then the road, and continue on the trail (follow the square symbol).

2.7 Come to a trail crossroads and continue straight ahead onto a connector trail (marked with a transparent square symbol).

3.0 At an unmarked trail junction, turn left.

3.1 Cross the road and take the trail marked with a triangle symbol.

3.2 Cross the road and continue on the trail (follow the triangle symbol).

3.3 Come to a Y and take the left fork (follow the triangle symbol).

3.6 Come to a Y and take the left fork (follow the triangle symbol).

3.7 Arrive back at the trailhead.

3 Point Defiance Park: Owen Beach– Boathouse–Japanese Garden Loop

This loop encompasses several of Point Defiance Park's best features in one relatively short hike: a popular beach, a shoreline promenade, the boathouse (a pleasure boater's hub in Tacoma), a formal Japanese garden, and a fern- and moss-draped forest of giant maples. This route intersects the trailhead for the route described in the Point Defiance Spine–Outer Loop–Inner Loop route, so the ambitious hiker wishing to spend an additional few hours on the trail can easily combine the two hikes.

Distance: 1.6-mile loop
Approximate hiking time: 1 hour
Difficulty: Moderate due to gradual inclines
Trail surface: Paved, dirt
Best season: Year-round
Other trail users: Skaters, bicycles
Canine compatibility: Leashed

dogs permitted
Fees and permits: No fees or permits required
Schedule: Daily, dawn to dusk
Maps: USGS Gig Harbor, WA; Tacoma street map
Trail contacts: Metro Parks Tacoma; (253) 305-1000; www .metroparkstacoma.org

Finding the trailhead: From I-5, take exit 132 onto WA 16. Take exit 3 (Sixth Avenue) off WA 16, and at the second stoplight turn right onto North Pearl Street. Stay on North Pearl Street (WA 163), which will end at Point Defiance Park. Drive into the park and follow the signs to Owen Beach. GPS: N47 18.76' / W 122 31.72'

The Hike

Owen Beach is a favorite gathering spot in Tacoma. Its popularity is not surprising given its natural setting: a pristine pebble beach strewn with driftwood and surrounded by hillsides of lush deep forest and with a broad view across the sound to Vashon Island. What better place to begin a hike?

As you are facing the water, take the promenade to the right past the kayak rental shop and concession stand. It follows the shoreline above the beach for about 0.5 mile to the boathouse. Views take in the mouth of Commencement Bay, home of the Port of Tacoma, and Brown Point with its lighthouse across the harbor.

Just past the boathouse, climb the stairs and cross the overpass, following the trail up a gradual incline heading away from the shore. Soon you will reach the Japanese garden and a pavilion. As an optional spur, walk to the left past the pavilion, where you will find the pond, an outstanding example of Japanese landscaping using a water feature. The trail continues to the right of the pavilion through the Japanese garden and across a short overpass to a picnic area and playground. Follow the trail along the top of the bluff until you reach a parking lot and the road.

Just past the parking lot, at the Rhododendron Garden sign, you will pass the trailhead for the route described in the Spine–Outer Loop–Inner Loop route. Optionally, if you wish to extend your hike by two hours and 3.6 miles, this makes a great additional segment through the park's extensive old-growth forest that delivers you back to this spot.

Continuing on the original route, the trail follows the road to the right through a shady grove of giant maples, a highlight of which is the abundance of ferns and mosses

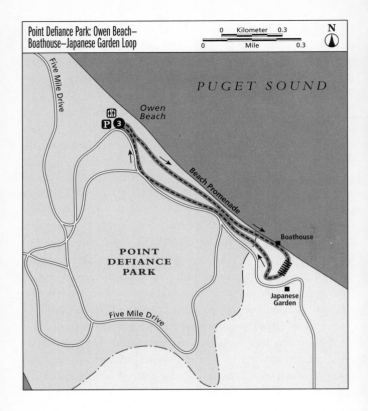

PUGET SOUND

Five Mile Drive

Owen
Beach

P ❸

Beach Promenade

Boathouse

POINT
DEFIANCE
PARK

Japanese
Garden

Five Mile Drive

covering the maples' trunks and branches, a feature common
in the Pacific Northwest temperate rain forests. Be careful
along this segment of trail since there is no barrier separating
the road from the pedestrian path other than a painted line,
and this is one of the park's most well-traveled roads. An
optional unmarked trail cuts through the woods to the right,
taking you away from the road and traffic.

Take the turnoff to Owen Beach and follow the road down the hill until you reach a dirt and wood stairway. Using the handrails and a great deal of caution, since this stairway is built on an uneven surface, follow it down to Owen Beach and the trailhead, completing the loop.

Miles and Directions

0.0   Facing the water, begin the hike on the promenade to the right of the parking lot.

0.6   Pass the boathouse and climb the stairs to the overpass; cross the overpass and follow the path.

0.7   You will reach the pavilion and Japanese garden; turn right at the first trail junction and walk through the garden to a pedestrian overpass.

0.8   Cross the overpass and turn right onto the dirt path that follows the top of the bluff through the picnic area and playground.

1.2   Cross the parking lot and turn right into the pedestrian/bike lane of Five Mile Drive. Supervise children and dogs closely since there is no traffic barrier here. (An alternative primitive trail enters the woods to the right shortly after the parking lot.)

1.4   Turn right at the road to Owen Beach; follow the pedestrian lane down the hill.

1.5   Turn right onto the stairs leading down to the beach. Caution: these primitive stairs are badly eroded; use the handrail.

1.6   Arrive back at the trailhead.

4 Tacoma Nature Center: Second Bridge Loop–Hillside Loop Trails

Tacoma Nature Center is the city's hub for education about all things natural, complete with exhibits with a knowledgeable staff on hand to answer questions. But what's hiding in the nearly sixty acres of woods and wetlands behind the visitor center? Snake Lake, 2 miles of trails, and dozens of species of mammals, birds, reptiles, and amphibians that call this place home.

Distance: 1.6-mile loop
Approximate hiking time: 1 hour
Difficulty: Moderate with some inclined segments
Trail surface: Dirt, gravel
Best season: Year-round
Other trail users: None
Canine compatibility: No animals permitted

Fees and permits: No fees or permits required
Schedule: The trail is open daily, 8:00 a.m. to dusk
Maps: USGS Tacoma South, WA; Tacoma street map
Trail contacts: Metro Parks Tacoma; (253) 305-1000; www .metroparkstacoma.org

Finding the trailhead: From southbound I-5, take exit 132, or from northbound I-5, take exit 133 onto WA 16. Take exit 1C off WA 16 and turn left onto South Center Street. Turn left onto South Tyler Street, take a right at the sign for Tacoma Nature Center, and park. The trailhead is at the kiosk outside the nature center. GPS: N47 14.54' / W122 29.61'

The Hike

The wetlands and forest surrounding Snake Lake (named for its shape) create a green oasis in the center of Tacoma.

The city acquired the site in the 1920s, and since then local conservationists have worked hard to preserve this crucial wetland habitat, recognizing it as a valuable asset in the heart of the city. The latest developments were the creation of the Tacoma Nature Center, an important resource for science education, and an expansion of park acreage.

The trails are a favorite among runners, day hikers, families out on a stroll, and classes of kids out on nature hikes. If you're there during the visitor center's open hours, you can stop inside and pick up a map for a self-guided nature walk, or download the maps from the Web site.

The trail begins at the kiosk outside the visitor center; a trail map is posted at the kiosk. The trail enters riparian forest with Snake Lake hidden behind the vegetation to the left. The lake is a long, shallow, narrow body of water, mostly covered with lily pads, cattails, and other aquatic plants, all great hiding places for the dozens of species that are often heard but not seen. You will also hear the roar of traffic from nearby Tyler Street and WA 16, which crosses over Snake Lake at its south end.

Follow the trail along the lake, pass the first bridge, and continue on to the second bridge. Turn left onto the bridge, which offers excellent views of the lake and wetlands. Cross the bridge. The trail will veer left along the lake, and in a short distance you will come to a junction for the Hillside Loop Trail. Turn right onto that trail as it switchbacks up the wooded hillside. Here the vegetation changes from wetland forest to a mature forest of fir, cedar, and hemlock, the three trees predominant in Pacific Northwest coniferous forests.

The trail is moderately steep in places, but it soon levels off on a ridge and then begins its descent. At the bottom

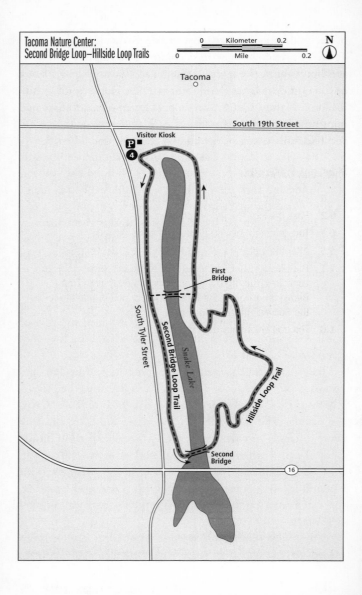

Tacoma Nature Center:
Second Bridge Loop–Hillside Loop Trails

0   Kilometer   0.2

0   Mile   0.2

N

Tacoma

South 19th Street

Visitor Kiosk

P

4

First
Bridge

South Tyler Street

Second Bridge Loop Trail

Snake Lake

Hillside Loop Trail

Second
Bridge

16

of the hill, turn right to rejoin the Second Bridge Loop Trail. You will come to First Bridge, a good place to enjoy another view of the lake, and hopefully spot great blue herons, wood ducks, hooded mergansers, or many of the other species on the lake. From First Bridge, turn around and rejoin the Second Bridge Loop Trail, following it to the left and back to the visitor center and the trailhead.

Miles and Directions

0.0 Begin at the kiosk next to the visitor center.

0.2 Pass the First Bridge trail junction.

0.4 Turn left onto Second Bridge and cross the lake.

0.5 After the bridge, take a right onto the Hillside Loop Trail.

1.1 The Hillside Loop Trail ends and rejoins the Second Bridge Loop Trail; turn right. Take an immediate left onto First Bridge for a view of the lake; backtrack and turn left to rejoin the Second Bridge Loop Trail.

1.6 The trail ends back at the kiosk.

5 Titlow Park

The property at Titlow Park was once home to Washington's first tidewater resort hotel, the Hotel Hesperides, which opened in 1911. Today, only a Swiss-style chalet known as Titlow Lodge remains and is used as a community center. Titlow Park's trails include a paved beach promenade at a popular diving spot (Titlow Beach Marine Preserve) and a route along a natural scenic shoreline and through acres of woods.

Distance: 1.3-mile loop
Approximate hiking time: 1 hour
Difficulty: Easy
Trail surface: Paved, bark chips, gravel, dirt
Best season: Year-round
Other trail users: None
Canine compatibility: Leashed dogs permitted

Fees and permits: No fees or permits required
Schedule: Open daily, dawn to dusk
Maps: USGS Gig Harbor, WA; USGS Steilacoom, WA; Tacoma street map
Trail contacts: Metro Parks Tacoma; (253) 305-1000; www.metroparkstacoma.org

Finding the trailhead: From I-5, take exit 132 onto WA 16. Take exit 4 (North Jackson Avenue). Turn left onto North Jackson Avenue and right at Sixth Avenue. Follow Sixth Avenue down the hill to the water. Titlow Park and the trailhead are at the west end of Sixth Avenue; parking is along the street or in the parking lot near the lodge and pool. GPS: N47 14.80' / W122 33.18'

The Hike

Tucked between the Narrows Bridge and Day Island in a beach community on Puget Sound known as Titlow Beach,

Tacoma's Titlow Park attracts everyone from scuba divers to Little League teams, beachcombers, and hikers. Views of the Narrows Bridge, Puget Sound, Kitsap Peninsula, and Fox Island make this beachfront park a great place to take in the stunning scenery the region offers.

Titlow Park is best hiked in a loop, beginning at the end of Sixth Avenue. Walk north (or right, facing the water) on the promenade that runs between the beach and the railroad tracks. The pilings just offshore are all that remains of a pier where steamers carrying passengers up and down Puget Sound once docked. This off-shore area is now the state-managed Titlow Beach Marine Preserve, a marine wildlife refuge popular with scuba divers.

The trail continues north as it passes through an easement belonging to BNSF Railway, becomes a service road, and enters the woods. At the first trail intersection after you enter the woods, turn left toward the shore. The trail shadows the shoreline and beach through a native forest, with access to secluded coves and beaches perfect for beachcombing at low tide. The trail passes a picnic shelter and eventually rejoins the service road. You will turn left onto the road and pass Tacoma Outboard Association, a private boaters' club, and come to a bridge. Cross the bridge, follow the road as it heads south through the woods, and take the first trail junction to the right. This trail continues through the woods, past the duck pond, playground, and Titlow Lodge Community Center, and ends at Sixth Avenue, the parking area, and the trailhead.

Miles and Directions

0.0 Begin the hike at the parking lot and walk along Sixth Avenue toward the water, cross the railroad track, and turn right to follow the paved shoreline promenade.

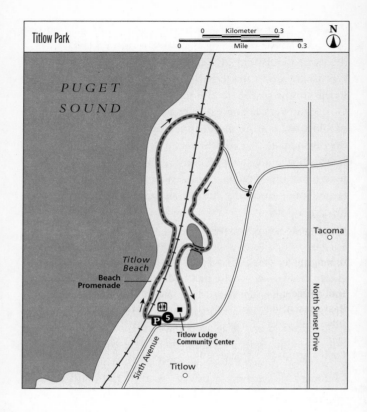

0.3 The trail enters the woods; turn left at the fork and follow the trail along the shoreline.

0.7 Turn left onto the service road and follow it across the bridge.

0.8 Turn right off the service road and onto the trail, which will pass through the woods to the left of the pond, right on a footbridge across the pond, and left past the playground and Titlow Lodge Community Center.

1.3 The trail ends back at the parking area on Sixth Avenue.

6 Grandview Trail-Soundview Trail

On the site of an abandoned gravel pit with one of the most stunning vistas of Puget Sound to be found, Chambers Bay Golf Course and surrounding park lands sprang up. What would such a property be without taking advantage of the hilly terrain and panoramic views for a multiuse public trail? These two trails, which together form a loop, are heavily used for many reasons.

Distance: 3.2-mile loop

Approximate hiking time: 1.5 to 2 hours

Difficulty: Moderate due to steep grade

Trail surface: Paved

Best season: Year-round

Other trail users: Skaters, bicycles

Canine compatibility: Leashed dogs permitted

Fees and permits: No fees or permits required

Schedule: Dawn to dusk, every day

Maps: USGS Steilacoom, WA; Tacoma street map

Trail contacts: Pierce County Parks and Recreation; (253) 798-4176; www.co.pierce.wa .us/pc/abtus/ourorg/ccp/Trails .htm

Finding the trailhead: From I-5, take exit 130 (56th Street) and head west. South 56th Street will become Cirque Drive west as you leave Tacoma and enter University Place. Follow Cirque Drive west to its end and turn right onto Grandview Drive. Circle around the first roundabout and reverse your direction on Grandview Drive. In a very short distance, turn right into the Chambers Bay North Meadow parking lot, where the trail begins. GPS N47 12.75' / W122 34.18'

The Hike

The Chambers Bay property that the Grandview and Soundview Trails traverse has a long history. Situated just up the beach from Steilacoom, Washington's first incorporated town, the land at Chambers Bay has been heavily exploited as a gravel pit that has produced some of the finest grade gravel in the world. Today, the property remains dotted with a few industrial ruins of the old gravel pit operation juxtaposed against a new, world-class golf course. The two paved trails, joined together, circle it all.

The route is a loop, so you can begin at any place you can park. The route described here begins at the North Meadow and follows the aptly named Grandview Trail along the top of the bluff above the golf course south for nearly a mile. From this trail, south Puget Sound opens up with the historic town of Steilacoom to the south and Hartstein, McNeil, Anderson, and Fox Islands to the west with the Olympic Mountains beyond.

At the main entrance to the golf course, the trail turns to the right, where it becomes Soundview Trail and continues down a long hill to a park at the Central Meadow. Here, circle the ruins of the old gravel operation and an expansive lawn and head north above the water. The trail cuts through the west edge of the golf course. Heed the signs warning you to dodge wayward golf balls.

At the north end of the course, your climb begins. The trail makes a right into the forest and heads sharply uphill, switches back, levels off, and heads uphill again. The elevation gains about 200 feet from where you enter the forest to the North Meadow at the top of the bluff—in the distance of roughly 0.5 mile.

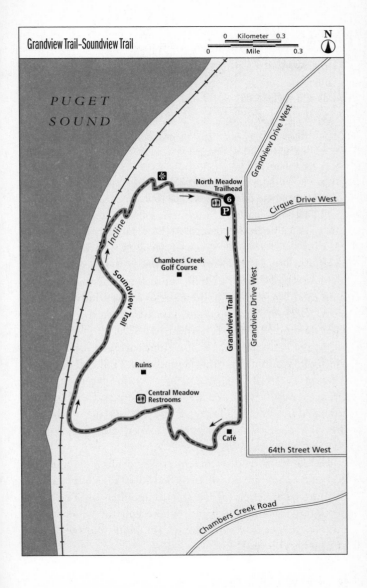

Grandview Trail–Soundview Trail

0   Kilometer   0.3
0   Mile   0.3

N

PUGET SOUND

Grandview Drive West

Cirque Drive West

Incline

Soundview Trail

Chambers Creek Golf Course

North Meadow Trailhead

6

P

Grandview Trail

Grandview Drive West

Ruins

Central Meadow Restrooms

Café

64th Street West

Chambers Creek Road

A viewpoint at the top of the bluff is a great place to sit and catch your breath and enjoy the view before closing the loop and returning to the trailhead.

Miles and Directions

0.0 Begin the Grandview Trail at the North Meadow parking lot. Begin walking south past the restrooms; the trail will parallel Grandview Drive West, which is on the other side of a narrow greenbelt.

0.8 Turn right at the sign for the Soundview Trail, follow the trail around the cafe, cross the golf course road, and continue down the hill.

1.3 At the Central Meadow parking lot and restrooms, turn left and follow the trail around the lawn toward the bluff.

2.0 Go through a trail junction and continue straight ahead; the trail enters the golf course.

2.3 The trail enters the woods and begins a moderately steep uphill grade.

2.8 Come to a viewpoint; the trail becomes the Grandview Trail again as it continues to the left.

3.2 Arrive back at the trailhead.

7 Scott Pierson Trail: War Memorial Park to Narrows Bridge

This hike crosses a regional landmark: the Tacoma Narrows Bridge. The original span opened in July 1940 and, four months later, a storm sent it oscillating wildly and plunging nearly 200 feet into water, earning it the name Galloping Gertie. Today, two spans carry traffic across the Narrows, the newest span with a lane for bicyclists and hikers that is a segment of the much longer Scott Pierson Trail, offering breathtaking views of Puget Sound.

Distance: 3.2 miles out and back

Approximate hiking time: 1.5 hours

Difficulty: Easy

Trail surface: Paved

Best season: Year-round

Other trail users: Bicycles

Canine compatibility: Leashed dogs permitted

Fees and permits: No fees or permits required

Schedule: Tacoma Narrows Bridge is open daily, 24 hours a day; War Memorial Park is open dawn to dusk daily

Maps: USGS Gig Harbor, WA; Tacoma street map

Trail contacts: City of Tacoma Public Works; (253) 594-7879; www.cityoftacoma.org; WSDOT (360) 705-7000; www.wsdot .wa.gov

Finding the trailhead: From I-5, take exit 132 onto WA 16. Take exit 4 (North Jackson Avenue). Turn left onto North Jackson Avenue, left onto Sixth Avenue, left onto North Skyline Drive, and an immediate left into the War Memorial Park parking lot. The trailhead is at the end of the lot. GPS: N47 15.38' / W122 32.06'

The Hike

The Scott Pierson Trail is a popular bike route that shadows WA 16 across Tacoma's west side, and some of its more scenic stretches are perfect for hikers. One such stretch—from War Memorial Park across the Tacoma Narrows Bridge and back—provides a short, easy hike, but one that can be challenging for anyone with a fear of heights.

The original Tacoma Narrows Bridge, aka Galloping Gertie, claimed infamy as the worst bridge engineering disaster in history, but now enjoys retirement on the National Register of Historic Places 30 fathoms under the sea as one of the world's largest man-made reefs. The only problem is that unless you're a diver or a fish, you won't get to see it.

The current bridge is actually two separate bridges: one that opened in 1950 to replace Galloping Gertie and one that opened in 2007 to alleviate traffic congestion. The 2007 Narrows Bridge span holds the pedestrian/bike path.

A park that honors veterans of the armed forces—War Memorial Park—sat directly in the path of the proposed new span, so the park was rebuilt at its current location with expansive lawns, flower gardens, and memorial plaques. War Memorial Park is a great place to begin your hike across the mile-long Narrows Bridge.

From the park's parking lot, follow the paved path down a gradual slope through the park until you reach the intersection of WA 16 and North Jackson Avenue. The pedestrian path crosses the intersection and continues on the approach to the bridge. Soon the bluff beneath the bridge vanishes, and the waters of the Narrows flow nearly 200 feet below through the only waterway connecting central and south Puget Sound.

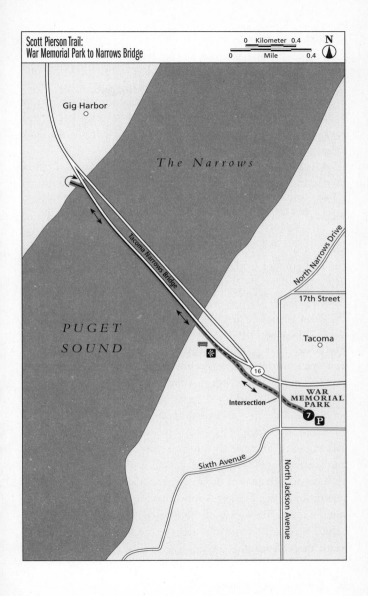

0   Kilometer   0.4

0   Mile   0.4

N

Gig Harbor

The Narrows

Tacoma Narrows Bridge

PUGET SOUND

North Narrows Drive

17th Street

Tacoma

16

WAR
MEMORIAL
PARK

7 P

Intersection

Sixth Avenue

North Jackson Avenue

The path is wide enough to safely accommodate bike traffic and pedestrians, but it parallels a lane of motorized traffic (separated by a cement barrier) so traffic noise on this busy bridge is a constant presence. But the thrill of crossing this engineering marvel and the expansive views up and down the sound make this unique and exciting hike well worth it.

Miles and Directions

0.0   The trail begins at the War Memorial Park parking lot. Walk into the park and follow the trail down the slope toward the bridge span.

0.2   Come to the intersection at North Jackson Avenue; cross the street with the pedestrian signal. Follow the pedestrian/bike path onto the bridge.

1.2   Reach the midpoint of the suspension bridge, a great place to pause and take in the view.

1.6   Reach the opposite end of the bridge span; turn around and backtrack.

3.2   The trail ends back at the War Memorial Park parking lot.

8 Nisqually National Wildlife Refuge: Twin Barns Loop

Rescued from the developers in the 1960s and 70s, this former dairy farm occupies the scenic Nisqually River Delta, a critical habitat for hundreds of wildlife species. More than 700 acres of the refuge are undergoing restoration work to return the estuaries to tidal influence. Miles of trails through extensive wetlands and Puget Sound tidelands draw hikers, birders, photographers, and painters—all there to witness nature in action.

Distance: 1.5-mile loop
Approximate hiking time: 1 hour
Difficulty: Easy, flat trail
Trail surface: Paved, wooden boardwalk
Best season: Year-round
Other trail users: None
Canine compatibility: Dogs prohibited
Fees and permits: No permits required; there is a vehicle fee, payable at the visitor center pay station.
Schedule: Daily, dawn to dusk
Maps: USGS Nisqually, WA; Washington State road map
Trail contacts: Nisqually National Wildlife Refuge; (800) 344-9453, (360) 753-9467; www.fws.gov/nisqually

Finding the trailhead: From Tacoma, drive south on I-5 and take exit 114. (From the exit, prominent signs lead to the Nisqually National Wildlife Refuge.) At the first traffic signal (Nisqually Cut-off Road SE), turn right, drive under the underpass, and turn right at the next intersection (Brown Farm Road NE). Follow the road to the visitor center and park; the trailhead is in front of the visitor center. GPS: N47 4.36' / W122 42.80'

The Hike

The Nisqually River originates on Mt. Rainier, cuts roughly an 80-mile path through the foothills, and empties into Puget Sound at Nisqually National Wildlife Refuge. Not far from the river's mouth, McAllister Creek empties into the sound as well; originally Medicine Creek, this was the site of the historic Medicine Creek Treaty of 1854. Framed by these two rivers and the sound, a vast network of wetlands, estuaries, forests, and tidelands are home to hundreds of migrating bird species and other wildlife.

The refuge has an impressive visitor center (open Wednesday through Sunday, 9:00 a.m. to 4:00 p.m.). If you're visiting during open hours, the visitor center's staff, exhibits, and bookstore can provide an excellent orientation to the refuge.

Facing the visitor center, begin the hike to the left. Follow the signs to the Twin Barns Loop Trail, a boardwalk above the wetlands offering overlooks, interpretive signs, and plenty of opportunities to spot birds and more elusive wetland wildlife, such as otter and mink.

At the trail junction near two enormous barns (remnants of the property's original dairy), take the spur trail to the left to the observation platform, where views stretch across the open wetlands to the tidelands of Puget Sound and to the islands and Olympic Mountains beyond.

Return to the Twin Barns Loop Trail and follow the sign to the left to continue the loop. The boardwalk crosses the wetlands and comes to another junction beside a service road. Turn left and follow the signed boardwalk to the Nisqually River Overlook for a view of the river as it snakes toward the sound. Retrace your steps back to the Twin Barns Loop Trail and follow it straight ahead. The board-

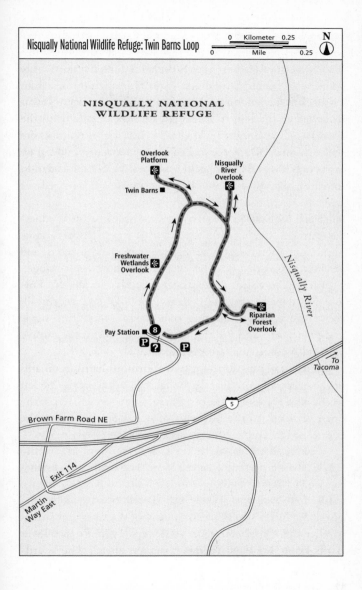

NISQUALLY NATIONAL
WILDLIFE REFUGE

Overlook
Platform

Twin Barns

Nisqually River
Overlook

Freshwater
Wetlands
Overlook

Riparian
Forest
Overlook

Pay Station

8

Nisqually River

To
Tacoma

5

Brown Farm Road NE

Exit 114

Martin
Way East

Nisqually National Wildlife Refuge: Twin Barns Loop

0   Kilometer   0.25

0   Mile   0.25

N

walk winds through forest and comes to another spur trail to the Riparian Forest Overlook. Turn left and follow this boardwalk spur leading a short distance to an overlook platform, where interpretive signs explain riparian forest life.

Back at the junction, a sign directs you to the visitor center to complete the loop. The refuge also has an extensive network of dike trails offering longer hikes; as the refuge proceeds with its Estuary Restoration Project, some of these dike trails are being demolished and new ones created, but the plan calls for no changes to the Twin Barns Loop Trail.

Miles and Directions

0.0 Facing the visitor center, begin the hike to the left in a clockwise direction; veer right and follow the TWIN BARNS LOOP TRAIL sign to the boardwalk.

0.2 Pass the Freshwater Wetlands Overlook.

0.4 Turn left at the trail junction; follow the sign to the observation platform.

0.5 Enter the observation platform; turn around and retrace your steps back to the last junction.

0.6 Turn left at the trail junction.

0.7 Turn left at the trail junction; follow the sign to the Nisqually River Overlook.

0.8 At the Nisqually River Overlook, turn around and retrace your steps back to the last trail junction, and at the junction continue straight ahead.

1.1 At the trail junction, turn left and follow the sign to the Riparian Forest Overlook.

1.2 From the Riparian Forest Overlook, retrace your steps back to the last trail junction.

1.3 At the trail junction, turn left and continue on to the trailhead.

1.5 Arrive back at the trailhead.

9 Swan Creek Trail

Seldom–visited Swan Creek Park is one of Tacoma's best-kept secrets. This undeveloped 322–acre stretch of land runs through a canyon with a wide creek bed at its floor and a virtual jungle of native trees, ferns, and wildflowers hugging the steep hillsides. Beside the creek, native vegetation, and wildlife, the main attraction in this park is the trail, making this shady, wooded canyon an urban hiker's paradise.

Distance: 4.0 miles out and back
Approximate hiking time: 3 hours
Difficulty: More challenging, with a 280-foot elevation gain
Trail surface: Dirt, boardwalk
Best season: Year-round, but the trail is muddy after a rain
Other trail users: None
Canine compatibility: Leashed dogs permitted
Fees and permits: No fees or permits required
Schedule: Open daily, dawn to dusk
Maps: USGS Tacoma South, WA; Tacoma street map
Trail contacts: Metro Parks Tacoma; (253) 305-1000; www.metroparkstacoma.org

Finding the trailhead: From I-5, take exit 135 and follow East 28th Street a short distance until it becomes a Y. The left fork is River Road East, and the right is Pioneer Way East. Take Pioneer Way East and turn right into Swan Creek Park. The trailhead is at the parking lot and kiosk. GPS: N47 13.68' / W122 23.42'

The Hike

Forgotten, neglected, and once in peril for acquisition as a landfill, the canyon that makes up Swan Creek Park is one of the region's biggest success stories, and one with a very happy ending—for hikers. Grassroots conservation groups rescued the land and have since dedicated themselves to cleaning up the park and restoring both the creek and forest habitats. Hikers should stay tuned to developments in this park. The City of Tacoma has approved funding for improvements to Swan Creek Park's trail and habitats through 2012.

The park's single trail offers easy hiking in some places and presents challenges in others. Begin the hike at the kiosk near the parking lot off Pioneer Way East. Follow the trail across the grassy field to the sediment pond, where it turns left and parallels the creek bed. In a short distance a footbridge crosses the creek, and the trail narrows and follows the right side of the creek into a once logged but now flourishing forest where, in springtime, native wildflowers abound.

The wooded hillsides rarely dry out, creating muddy spots even long after a rain, but raised boardwalks carry hikers above the muck in the wettest areas. The narrow, primitive trail begins its ascent, gradually in places and steeply in others. The hillsides occasionally give way to mudslides, causing damage to the trail and requiring frequent maintenance. One particularly challenging stretch climbs a set of old stairs built into the hillside but badly damaged by storm water. Good treads, trekking poles, drinking water, and serious attention to trail safety will help ensure a rewarding experience on this trail.

The Swan Creek Trail ascends roughly 300 feet to the rim of the canyon where an old homestead once stood and ends 2 miles from its starting point at East 56th Street. There, you will turn around and retrace your steps back to the canyon floor.

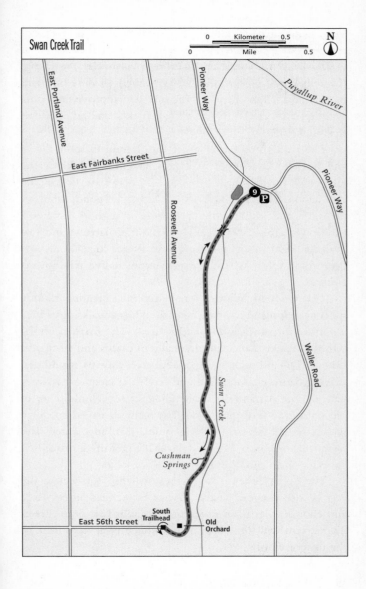

Swan Creek Trail

Miles and Directions

0.0 The trailhead begins at the parking lot and kiosk. Follow the trail back to the creek and follow it to the left (south) along the creek.

0.2 A footbridge crosses the creek.

0.6 At a fork in the trail, follow the main trail to the right up the hill.

1.3 Pass concrete bunkers protecting the natural springs that supply much of Swan Creek's water.

2.0 Turn around at the trail's end at East 56th Street and retrace your steps.

4.0 The trail ends back at the trailhead.

10 West Hylebos Wetlands Park

Preserving West Hylebos Wetlands as a park was an exercise in perseverance and hard labor launched by a few tenacious conservationists in the midst of 1980s urban growth. A battle ensued. The score: Opposition 0, Nature 1. The end result is one of the finest wetland parks in the Northwest. What better place to enjoy an easy day hike?

Distance: 1.7-mile loop and spur trails

Approximate hiking time: 1 hour

Difficulty: Easy

Trail surface: Gravel, boardwalk, dirt

Best season: Year-round

Other trail users: None

Canine compatibility: No pets allowed

Fees and permits: No fees or permits required

Schedule: Open daily, dawn to dusk

Maps: USGS Poverty Bay, WA; Tacoma/Pierce County street map

Trail contacts: City of Federal Way; (253) 835-6901; www .cityoffederalway.com. Friends of Hylebos, www.hylebos.org.

Finding the trailhead: From I-5, take exit 142B (South 348th Street). Drive west on South 348th Street and turn left at Fourth Avenue South into West Hylebos Wetlands Park; the trailhead is located at the parking lot. GPS: N47 17.38' / W122 19.75'

The Hike

A homesteader's log cabin (circa 1890) greets hikers at the trailhead at West Hylebos Wetlands Park. A period photo posted at the cabin depicts the scene when the cabin was first erected: a hewn log structure surrounded by the stumps of old-growth trees. But walk past the clearing and in a short time find yourself descending into a wetland forest, a verdant place that seems as though it has never seen the blade of a saw. But that's not true—most of the forest is second growth with the exception of a few old-growth trees.

In the wetland portion of the park, the entire trail is on newly constructed raised boardwalk taking hikers deep into this unique ecosystem. If you don't know the difference between "emergent" and "open-water" wetlands, or a Sitka spruce and a western hemlock, by the time you leave the park you will. Well-written interpretive signs along the trail provide those who wish to pause and learn an excellent environmental education. Overlooks along the route are great places to stop and take in some of the park's most notable features, such as a 600-year-old, 175-foot-tall Sitka spruce and the Deep Sink, a 30-foot-deep peat bog.

Two spur trails lead to small secluded lakes: Brooklake and Marlake, with excellent opportunities for spotting some of the wetlands' waterfowl. The Brooklake spur branches off from the Wetlands Loop Trail, and the Marlake spur begins midway between the trailhead and the Wetlands Loop.

Back at the trailhead, another prominent feature of the park, and a bit of a curiosity, is the Denny Cabin, moved from its original location in the heart of Seattle. In 1889 David Denny, one of Seattle's first settlers and entrepreneurs, built the two-story log cabin to house his real estate business in this new territory where land was up for grabs. Only a few months after it was built, Seattle's Great Fire of 1889 consumed most of the buildings in downtown Seattle, but the Denny Cabin somehow survived unscathed.

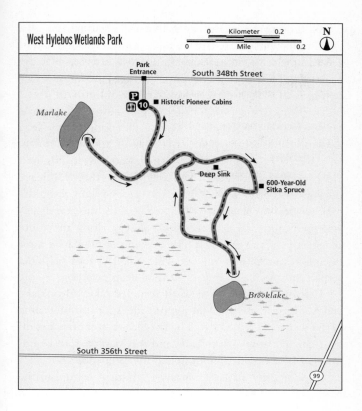

West Hylebos Wetlands Park

Park Entrance

South 348th Street

Marlake

P ⛹ 10 ■ Historic Pioneer Cabins

■ Deep Sink

■ 600-Year-Old Sitka Spruce

Brooklake

South 356th Street

99

Miles and Directions

0.0 The trailhead is at the Barker Cabin beside the parking lot.

0.2 Pass the signed junction with the Marlake spur trail; continue straight ahead.

0.4 Come to the Wetlands Loop Trail Y; follow the left fork and in a short distance pass the Deep Sink overlook.

0.5 Pass a 600-year-old Sitka spruce.

0.7 At the signed trail junction, turn left for the spur trail to Brooklake.

0.8 Arrive at the Brooklake overlook; turn around and return to the loop trail.

0.9 At the loop trail intersection, turn left and follow the exit sign.

1.1 At the trail junction, turn left.

1.2 At the signed trail junction, turn left to follow the spur trail to Marlake.

1.3 Arrive at Marlake; turn around and return to the main trail.

1.5 At the main trail, turn left.

1.7 Arrive back at the trailhead.

11 Spanaway Park Trail

This popular 135–acre multiuse park located 10 miles south of Tacoma occupies the northeastern shore of Spanaway Lake and has long been a favorite outdoor recreation spot in Pierce County. With the exception of the park, this 280–acre lake is surrounded by residential properties. The park's paved trail follows the lakeshore and returns through the upper area of the park in an easy loop hike that's suitable for any ability.

Distance: 1.5-mile loop
Approximate hiking time: 1 hour
Difficulty: Easy
Trail surface: Paved
Best season: Year-round
Other trail users: Bicycles, skaters
Canine compatibility: Leashed dogs permitted
Fees and permits: No fees or permits required
Schedule: Open daily, 7:30 a.m. to dusk, with restricted hours in December and early January due to Fantasy Lights, a drive-through holiday light display. Call or see Web site for specifics.
Maps: USGS Spanaway, WA; Tacoma street map
Trail contacts: Pierce County Parks and Recreation; (253) 798-4176; www.co.pierce.wa .us/PC/

Finding the trailhead: From I-5, take exit 127 (WA 512). Take the Pacific Avenue exit (WA 7) off WA 512 and drive south to Military Road South. Turn right onto Military Road South and left into Spanaway Park. As you are facing the park entrance, the trailhead is at the beginning of the first parking lot. GPS: N47 7.29' / W122 26.77'

The Hike

Various theories explain how Spanaway got its name. The one that seems to have gained the widest acceptance comes from the days when a railway ran from Tacoma to nearby Mt. Rainier. The distance between Tacoma and the town then known as Lake Park, a stop on the line, was about 10 miles, or one "span" in railroad lingo. Tacoma was said to be a "span away," so Lake Park became known as Spanaway at around the turn of the twentieth century.

Spanaway Park includes 135 acres of lakeshore, expansive lawns, swimming beaches, picnic areas, and more, all set beneath a canopy of giant conifers. The paved trail begins at the park's north entrance at the north parking lot. Follow the trail south along the lakeshore, a protected area here resembling a pond with irises and lily pads, and continue south where the lake opens up. Shoreline restoration on this lake is fortunately a priority with the county, so you might find the shoreline in varying states of repair in places.

You will pass two swimming beaches that are lifeguard-free, so if you're compelled to cool off with a dip, do so with caution. You will also pass a boathouse and pavilion, a great place to pause and enjoy views of the lake or rent a canoe and get in some paddling.

At the south end of the park, the trail climbs a gentle slope, loops around to the left, and returns via the upper area of the park, where you will pass picnic areas and a playground. If you wish to extend your hike, an optional spur trail near the trailhead veers off to the left past a picnic shelter and restrooms, crosses a footbridge, climbs a small hill, and explores a natural wooded area.

Miles and Directions

0.0 The trailhead is located at the first parking lot inside the park entrance; follow the paved trail down the slope, past the restrooms and picnic shelter, and along the lakeshore.

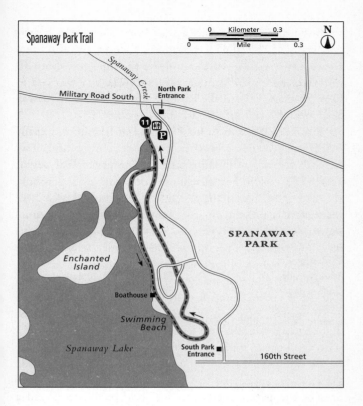

0.1 At the trail fork, turn right and follow the lakeshore.

0.6 Pass the boathouse and ramp.

0.7 You come to the end of the park where the trail loops to the left away from the shore and goes north through the upper park.

1.2 At a trail fork, go left toward the lakeshore trail.

1.3 Rejoin the lakeshore trail and follow it to the right (north) past the restrooms and toward the parking lot.

1.5 The trail ends at the parking lot.

12 Bresemann Forest

Once you walk beneath the arch that announces you have entered Bresemann Forest, you step beneath a canopy of towering firs surrounded by a lush understory. You discover a rushing creek with a channel built just for returning salmon. You step deep into the forest, calmed by silence that's a welcome contrast to the haste of the urban world just beyond the gate.

Distance: 1.1-mile loop
Approximate hiking time: 45 minutes
Difficulty: Easy
Trail surface: Dirt
Best season: Year-round
Other trail users: Bicycles
Canine compatibility: Leashed dogs permitted

Fees and permits: No fees or permits required
Schedule: Open daily, dawn to dusk
Maps: USGS Spanaway, WA; Tacoma street map
Trail contacts: Pierce County Parks and Recreation; (253) 798-4176; www.co.pierce.wa .us/PC/

Finding the trailhead: From I-5, take exit 127 (WA 512). Take the Pacific Avenue exit (WA 7) off WA 512 and drive south to Military Road South. Turn right onto Military Road South, right onto C Street South, and make the first left into the Sprinker Recreation Center parking lot. The signed trailhead is at the west side of the parking lot. GPS: N47 7.33' / W122 26.55'

The Hike

To hike through Bresemann Forest, you'd never guess it was once a prairie and not a forest at all. Some native trees began to take root in the grassland more than three centuries ago, but most of the trees in this lush forest—primarily Douglas fir—are roughly one hundred years old. Pierce County Parks and Recreation acquired the property in 1961 from a private owner and transitioned it to a park with a network of nature trails.

The forest is fenced in, so it's virtually impossible to get lost regardless of which trail you take. The route described in this chapter circles the forest in a clockwise loop.

As you enter the forest, traffic noise from nearby Military Road is noticeable, but as you move farther along the trail, the rush of traffic is replaced by an occasional birdsong interrupting the silence. Shortly after you enter the park, turn left onto a side trail that approaches Spanaway Creek. Follow the flow of the creek (to the right) until you come to a footbridge crossing the fish channel where metal sculptures of salmon adorn a concrete wall above the channel. Farther on, across the bridge, you will come to Bresemann Dam and a millpond. In 1873 the property owners, a family who ran a furniture factory, built the original dam out of logs, but inadvertently blocked salmon from returning upstream to spawn for more than a century. The dam was later rebuilt in 1953 with more durable material to prevent trout from escaping Spanaway Lake, which lies upstream, but with no regard for restoring salmon habitat. As recently as 2007, a salmon-friendly channel was dug through the forest, bypassing the dam, once again allowing spawning salmon to follow their natural route.

Beyond the dam, you will cross another bridge and follow the trail up a slight slope to reconnect with the main trail, which you will follow to the left. The trail loops

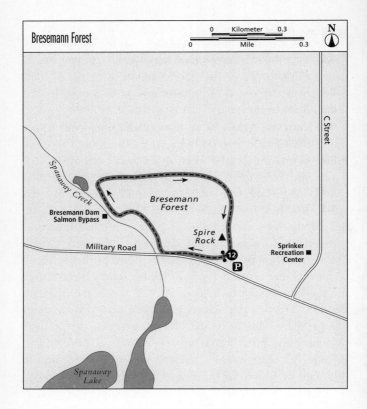

around to the right, follows the perimeter of the property, and opens up into a grassy area, Spire Rock (a rock climbing facility), and eventually the original parking lot where you began the hike. Other optional trails lead into the interior of the forest, inviting exploration and a longer hike.

Miles and Directions

0.0 The trailhead is located at the signed gate on the west side of the Sprinker Recreation Center parking lot.

0.1 At the trail fork, go left for a clockwise loop.

0.3 At the trail intersection, turn left and follow the creek.

0.4 Cross the bridge at the fish bypass channel and continue on the path to Bresemann Dam.

0.5 At the trail intersection before the fence, turn right and follow the trail along the edge of the forest to an open grassy field.

1.0 Pass Spire Rock and continue to the parking lot.

1.1 The trail ends at the parking lot.

13 Nathan Chapman Memorial Trail

In a community southeast of Tacoma known as South Hill, the Nathan Chapman Memorial Trail cuts through woods and wetlands, joining South Hill Park with a public athletic complex known as Heritage Recreation Center. The trail is a wide, paved route that connects to a loop trail at South Hill Park. This hike includes both the Nathan Chapman Memorial Trail and the South Hill Park Loop, together making one of the area's best short day hikes.

Distance: 2.2 miles out and back with loop

Approximate hiking time: 1 hour

Difficulty: Easy

Trail surface: Paved

Best season: Year-round

Other trail users: Bicyclists, skaters

Canine compatibility: Leashed dogs permitted

Fees and permits: No fees or permits required

Schedule: Open daily, dawn to dusk

Maps: USGS Puyallup, WA; Tacoma/Pierce County street map

Trail contacts: Pierce County Parks and Recreation; (253) 798-4176; www.co.pierce.wa .us/PC/

Finding the trailhead: From I-5, take exit 127 (WA 512). Drive east on WA 512, exit on 94th Avenue East, drive south to 144th Street East, and turn right. Turn right onto 86th Avenue East and take another right into the South Hill Park parking lot. The well-signed trailhead is on the north end of the lot. GPS: N47 7.70' / W122 18.88'

The Hike

Sergeant First Class Nathan Chapman was a local resident who served in the army for more than twelve years and was killed in action in Afghanistan. This trail is named after this highly respected, fallen hero; at the trailhead, a commemorative inscription tells his story.

The trail begins in wetlands with a footbridge crossing into second-growth forest. Maples, elderberry, salmonberry, and blooming wildflowers (in the spring) provide a lush understory typical of Pacific Northwest native forests. This trail is an excellent place to bring the binoculars for bird and butterfly watching, and your favorite bird and plant field guides to conduct your own nature hike.

Stay to the left as you pass two trail junctions to remain on the Nathan Chapman Memorial Trail. Soon you will cross a long curved footbridge over more wetlands before passing through a greenbelt with the South Hill community visible beyond the wetlands and woods on each side.

The trail ends at the Heritage Recreation Center, a sprawling complex of athletic facilities. Turn around at this point and retrace your steps. At the first trail junction you come to, turn left to join the South Hill Loop, a short trail through a beautiful stretch of forest. At the south end of the loop, the trail enters an open, grassy field and, at the next trail junction, loops to the right past picnic tables before reentering the forest. At the next junction, turn left to rejoin the Nathan Chapman Memorial Trail and return to the trailhead.

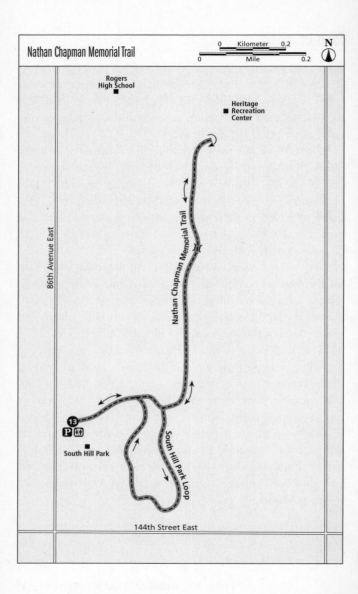

Nathan Chapman Memorial Trail

0   Kilometer   0.2

0   Mile   0.2

N

Rogers High School

Heritage Recreation Center

86th Avenue East

Nathan Chapman Memorial Trail

13

P

South Hill Park

South Hill Park Loop

144th Street East

Miles and Directions

0.0   The well-marked trailhead is located at the north end of the parking lot at South Hill Park.

0.2   Pass two trail junctions, one after another, and take the left fork at each junction.

0.8   At the athletic fields, turn around and return.

1.4   At the trail junction, turn left onto the loop trail.

1.8   At the trail junction in the open field, turn right to continue the loop trail.

2.0   At the trail junction, turn left to return to the trailhead.

2.2   Arrive back at the trailhead.

14 Foothills Trail: Orting

The Foothills Trail sits atop an historic railroad bed and snakes through the river valley southeast of Tacoma. This 25-mile-long trail is a popular commuter route and recreational destination for bicyclists, while hikers enjoy shorter, more manageable segments of the trail. One of the most scenic sections, best hiked on a clear day for the unobstructed views of nearby Mt. Rainier, begins in Orting and follows the Carbon River upstream through farmland and forest.

Distance: 4.6 miles out and back

Approximate hiking time: 2 to 3 hours

Difficulty: Easy, flat trail

Trail surface: Paved

Best season: Year-round

Other trail users: Bicyclists, skaters

Canine compatibility: Leashed dogs permitted

Fees and permits: No fees or permits required

Schedule: Open daily, dawn to dusk

Maps: USGS Orting, WA; Tacoma/Pierce County street map

Trail contacts: Pierce County Parks and Recreation; (253) 798-4176; www.co.pierce.wa .us/PC/

Finding the trailhead: From I-5, take exit 127 (WA 512). Drive east on WA 512 until it ends and becomes WA 167. Take the exit onto WA 167 North. Follow WA 167 and exit onto WA 410. Follow WA 410 and take the WA 162 exit. Turn right and follow WA 162 to Orting. In Orting, turn right at Orting Park on Calistoga Street West and take the first left and park. The trailhead is in the park. Facing the park from the parking area, follow Foothills Trail to the right. GPS: N47 5.85' / W122 12.28'

The Hike

Mt. Rainier erupted 500 years ago and sent a 50-foot-deep mudflow down the valley to the northwest all the way to what today is Tacoma. Over time, the long, wide swath of mud settled and became a fertile valley; the Puyallup and Carbon Rivers, which originate on Mt. Rainier glaciers, flow off the mountain and converge on the valley floor southeast of Tacoma.

The pioneer town of Orting was founded in 1889 near the convergence of the two rivers and became an agricultural hub. In recent years, many of the valley's farms have made way for housing developments to accommodate Tacoma's suburban expansion.

The 14,410-foot mountain towers above the valley, a majestic and breathtaking presence from nearly every vantage point. Gazing at the glacier-clad peak, it's easy to forget that it's still an active volcano and one day the disaster of 500 years ago will in all probability be repeated. If Rainier erupts, scientists predict the mudflow would reach the town of Orting within a half hour. A sophisticated warning system has been installed throughout the valley, and evacuation drills are a way of life.

Now that you are prepared in the event of an unlikely disaster, the Foothills Trail in Orting offers one of the region's easiest and most scenic day hikes. Beginning at the trailhead in the city park, follow the trail southeast. The trail cuts through town before skirting a farm where grazing cattle keep an eye on the bike and foot traffic passing by. Soon the trail joins the bank of the Carbon River, swift in this area as it rushes down the valley, and crosses a trestle where a creek empties into the river. Benches along this

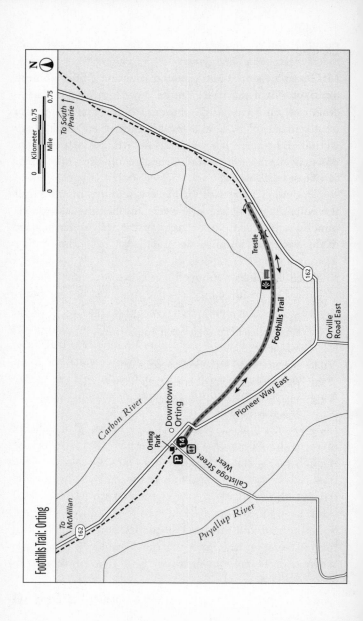

Foothills Trail: Orting

To South
Prairie

Trestle

Foothills Trail

162

Orville
Road East

Pioneer Way East

Carbon River

Downtown
Orting

Orting Park

P

Calistoga Street
West

To McMillan

162

Puyallup River

N

Kilometer   0.75

0

Mile

0

stretch allow great spots to pause and enjoy the river and foothills scenery.

Continue on as the trail enters a forest before rejoining the river. Mt. Rainier—15 miles away in a straight line—dominates the head of the valley, in many places completely unobstructed. Where the trail joins the highway, turn around and retrace your steps back to Orting. Optionally, you may continue on; the trail parallels a highway for much of the distance upriver and crosses several trestles offering scenic views. The trail segment between Orting and South Prairie is 11 miles one way, so if you extend your hike, be mindful of distance and the fact that you still have to return to the trailhead.

Miles and Directions

0.0 The trailhead and information kiosk is located at Orting City Park on North Washington Avenue and Calistoga Street West; facing North Washington Avenue, follow the Foothills Trail to the right.

0.6 The trail leaves Orting and passes a farm.

1.0 The trail joins the bank of the Carbon River.

1.3 The trail crosses a trestle and continues on through forest before rejoining the river.

2.3 The trail joins the highway; turn around and retrace your steps back to Orting.

4.6 Arrive back at the trailhead.

15 Flaming Geyser State Park

Unsuspecting visitors to Flaming Geyser State Park might expect to marvel at water and steam spouting from the earth in an Old Faithful–like display. Instead, they find a tiny flame powered by a natural methane seep. While it is an interesting geological feature, most visitors quickly turn to other pleasures, such as enjoying their picnic, casting a line in one of the state's top steelhead rivers or exploring the park's trails.

Distance: 1.4-mile loop

Approximate hiking time: 1 hour

Difficulty: Moderate due to a few short, steep grades

Trail surface: Dirt

Best season: Year-round

Other trail users: None

Canine compatibility: Leashed dogs permitted

Fees and permits: No fees or permits required

Schedule: Open daily, year-round, 8:00 a.m. to dusk

Maps: USGS Black Diamond, WA; Washington State map

Trail contacts: Washington State Parks (360) 902-8844; www .parks.wa.gov

Finding the trailhead: From I-5, take exit 142A onto WA 18 East. Just past Auburn, take the Southeast Auburn-Black Diamond Road exit, and an almost immediate right turn onto Southeast Green Valley Road. After approximately 8 miles, take a right turn onto Southeast Flaming Geyser Road, which enters the state park. The trailhead is located at a small parking area on the right before the main picnic and parking area at the end of the road. GPS: N47 16.50' / W122 1.90'

The Hike

In the Green River valley northeast of Tacoma, Flaming Geyser State Park has long been a favorite recreation spot for locals. While the little flame gets headline billing, it's the park's setting on the Green River with its nearby gorge that's the real draw. A large, popular picnic area, river access for kayakers, rafters, and anglers, and a network of trails bring people back again and again.

Each of the park's main trails is fairly short. A Geyser Trail just beyond the kiosk at the main trailhead passes the methane flame and climbs a short hill in a loop past the Bubbling Geyser, the River Trail follows along the river on the eastern side of the park, and the Ridge Trail climbs the ridge in a loop through dense lowland forest. The route described in this chapter is the Ridge Trail. (The River and Geyser Trails had sustained significant washouts in winter storms and were temporarily closed when this chapter was researched.)

The Ridge Trail begins with a steep climb, but within 0.1 mile it levels out and meanders through a forest dominated by moss- and fern-laden maples. In the rainy season, the narrow trail tends to be soggy, and maneuvering the muddy patches can be challenging. The trail is passable year-round but driest in late spring through early fall. Winter storms can do significant damage in the area, so it's always a good idea to call the state park office or visit the Web site to check on trail closures due to storm damage.

The trail follows the wooded ridge with a few ups and downs before beginning a sharp descent back to the valley floor. Once in the valley, you can cross the road into the picnic area and head left back to the trailhead.

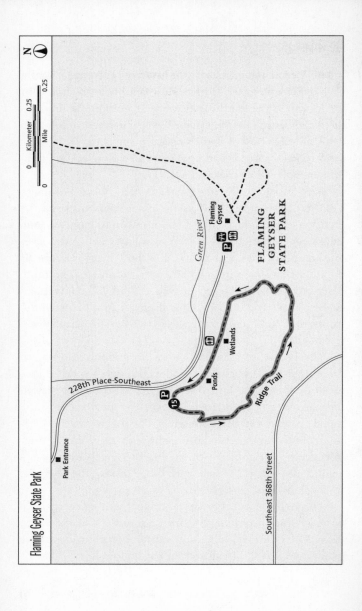

Flaming Geyser State Park

N

Park Entrance

228th Place–Southeast

Green River

Flaming
Geyser

FLAMING
GEYSER
STATE PARK

Wetlands

Ponds

15

Ridge Trail

Southeast 368th Street

Kilometer   0.25
0

Mile   0.25
0

Miles and Directions

0.0 The trailhead is located at the back of a small gravel parking area beside a pond on the right before the main parking and picnic areas. The trail starts out with a steep ascent.

0.2 Come to an unmarked trail junction and take the left trail.

0.7 The trail begins a steep descent.

0.9 The trail joins the park road; turn left and walk past the ponds and wetlands.

1.4 Arrive back at the trailhead.

16 Mud Mountain Dam Recreation Area: Rim Trail

When Mud Mountain Dam was completed in 1948, it held title as the largest earthen dam in the world. Its purpose is not to generate power but to restrain the potentially devastating force of the White River as it rushes along its course from Mt. Rainier's massive Emmons Glacier. Besides constructing the dam, the US Army Corps of Engineers also created a recreation area around the dam, complete with hiking trails.

Distance: 4.0 miles out and back

Approximate hiking time: 2 hours

Difficulty: Moderate

Trail surface: Dirt, gravel, boardwalk

Best season: Spring, summer, and fall; check trail conditions in winter.

Other trail users: Mountain bikers

Canine compatibility: Leashed dogs permitted

Fees and permits: No fees or permits required

Schedule: The park's hours vary seasonally; call or check the Web site for open days and hours.

Maps: USGS Enumclaw, WA; Washington State map

Trail contacts: US Army Corps of Engineers; (360) 825-3211; www.nws.usace.army .mil/PublicMenu/Menu.cfm? sitename=MM&pagename=Tour

Finding the trailhead: From I-5, take exit 127 (WA 512). Drive east on WA 512 until it ends and becomes WA 167. Take the WA 167 North exit. Follow WA 167 and exit onto WA 410. Follow WA 410 through the towns of Buckley and Enumclaw, turn right into the Mud Mountain Dam Recreation Area, and park in the designated parking area. GPS: N47 8.70' / W121 56.05'

The Hike

On this foothills trail, hikers experience a variety of terrain and vegetation, from maple and birch forests to giant stands of Douglas fir and cedar. The trail follows the rim of the canyon through a deep, verdant forest with a thick understory and the turbulent White River rushing far below on the canyon floor. A great season to hike this trail is mid- or late spring when shade-loving wildflowers are in full show in the forest.

The nearby 432-foot-high Mud Mountain Dam is not visible from the trail. For a good view of the dam, visit the viewpoint inside the park or the dam's interpretive center.

The well-signed Rim Trail begins just outside the Mud Mountain Dam Recreation Area's gate. Park inside the park and follow the gravel path (outside the park) along the chain link fence to the canyon rim. The trail leads to the left along the rim and offers some peek-a-boo views of the river. It's best not to tempt fate by going off trail for a better view—it's a long, steep tumble to the riverbed. On part of the trail, fences have been installed for your safety, and signs warn hikers to stay on the correct side of them.

In the rainy season, the trail presents some challenging swampy sections. Even though the Rim Trail is a relatively easy one, a few short steep grades add to the challenge for some hikers. You'll be glad you brought good hiking shoes and trekking poles.

Most trail junctions are well marked, but a few might leave you guessing. When in doubt, follow the route closest to the rim to stay on track. Exactly 2 miles from the trailhead, the Rim Trail joins a gravel road and begins its descent to the river. If you wish to add a few more miles to

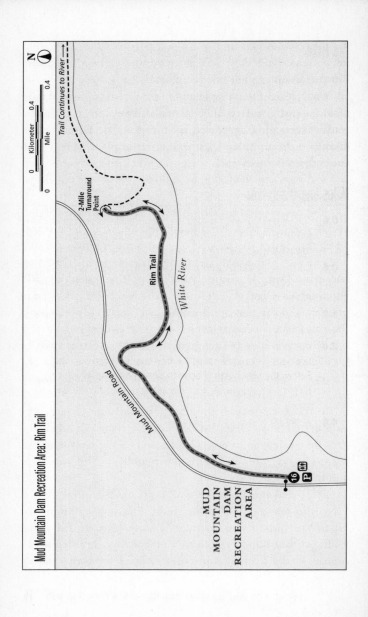

Mud Mountain Dam Recreation Area: Rim Trail

N

2-Mile
Turnaround
Point

Rim Trail

White River

Mud Mountain Road

MUD
MOUNTAIN
DAM
RECREATION
AREA

16
P

Trail Continues to River →

0   Kilometer   0.4

0   Mile   0.4

the hike, you may continue on that portion of the trail. But for a hike of moderate length and low elevation gain, you should turn around at this point.

The pleasant park inside the gate at Mud Mountain Dam Recreation Area offers picnic shelters and a children's wading pool and playground, so if it's a warm day and your hiking companions are kids, this is a great place to let them cool off after the hike.

Miles and Directions

0.0 The signed trailhead is located just outside the park's gate; follow the gravel path along the fence (outside the park) toward the canyon rim and turn left onto the Rim Trail.

0.6 Come to a junction with a narrow dirt road; turn right onto the road, walk a short distance, and turn left onto the marked trail.

1.2 Come to a junction; turn right and take an almost immediate left onto the marked trail.

2.0 Come to a junction with a gravel road that descends to the river; a sign indicates that the trail continues on the road. Follow the sign if you choose to descend to the river for a longer hike; otherwise, turn around and return to the trailhead.

4.0 Arrive back at the trailhead.

17 Federation Forest State Park

This more than 600-acre tract of riverfront old-growth forest was somehow spared the axe in a region that has been, and still is, heavily logged. It was dedicated as a state park in 1949, and the state continued to accumulate parcels until 1971. Today, a network of interpretive trails, the remnants of the Naches Trail (an early Native American route and later a pioneer trail), and other hiking trails crisscross the park for hikers of all abilities to enjoy.

Distance: 4.5 miles out and back plus loop
Approximate hiking time: 3 hours
Difficulty: Moderate
Trail surface: Dirt, boardwalk
Best season: Spring, summer, and fall; expect mud on some trails in spring and late fall
Other trail users: None
Canine compatibility: Leashed dogs permitted

Fees and permits: No fees or permits required
Schedule: Open daily, 8:00 a.m. to dusk, year-round with occasional closures in winter. Call or check the Web site for seasonal closures.
Maps: USGS Greenwater, WA; Washington State map
Trail contacts: Washington State Parks; (360) 902-8844; www.parks.wa.gov

Finding the trailhead: From I-5, take exit 127 (WA 512). Drive east on WA 512 until it ends and becomes WA 167. Take the WA 167 North exit. Follow WA 167 and exit onto WA 410. Follow WA 410 through the towns of Buckley and Enumclaw and turn right into the Federation Forest State Park parking area. GPS: N47 9.12' / W121 41.30'

The Hike

For the number and size of its old-growth trees, Federation Forest State Park presents one of the finest examples of virgin forest in the Pacific Northwest. The interpretive signs that educate hikers about the trees, native plants, and geologic and historic features only enhance the experience.

The park is located along a stretch of the White River, which originates on nearby Mt. Rainier's Emmons Glacier. Several trails meander through the park on both sides of WA 410. The best place to begin a visit to Federation Forest is at the park's Catherine Montgomery Interpretive Center with exhibits about the area's geology, flora, and fauna. Informational brochures and maps are available in the center, and staff is usually on hand to answer any questions.

The route described here remains on the river side of the highway in an area called Deadman Flat. It begins at the right of the interpretive center, and follows the West Trail, Greenlees Grove, Hobbit Trail, Wind in the Woods Trail, the historic Naches Trail, and, finally, the East Trail.

This is a dense, shady forest, in which the crowns of the old-growth trees hundreds of feet above the forest floor heavily filter all light and provide the perfect environment for shade- and moisture-loving plants, such as wild red huckleberry, salal, and Oregon grape. In spring the park is thick with shade-loving wildflowers in bloom, such as trillium, corydalis, and false lily of the valley.

The best season to hike Federation Forest is in the summer after the trails have had a chance to dry out. In spring and fall, it is unlikely that you will encounter poor trail conditions on the West and East Trails—the park's main interpretive trails—but other trails, such as Hobbit Trail (so

Federation Forest State Park

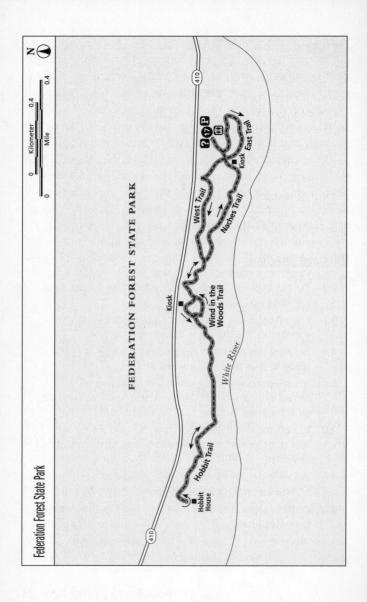

named for a whimsical and well-decorated makeshift "hobbit house" in a stump along the trail), can be extremely muddy and require hikers to skirt the trail in several places. Sections have boardwalks, but others do not. You'll be grateful for good treads and trekking poles.

Throughout the park, giant trees resting on the forest floor give testimony to the fierce power of the wind that rips through the Cascade foothills. Toppled trees sometimes block trails, cutting the route short. The state does its best to clear storm and flood debris from the most popular trails in a timely manner, but on some less-traveled trails, delayed cleanup can leave us a reminder of the forces of nature.

Miles and Directions

0.0 The trail begins at the right of the interpretive center, where free trail maps are available.

0.1 You will come to a kiosk with a trail map and interpretive information; continue on to the signed West Trail.

0.8 The West Trail ends at a trail junction; continue straight ahead to pass through Greenlees Grove.

1.0 You will come to a trail junction with another kiosk and posted trail map. This is the end of the West Trail; continue on in the same direction onto the Hobbit Trail.

2.0 You will come to the Hobbit House; turn around and retrace your steps, or continue on for a longer hike, trail conditions permitting.

3.0 Return to the trail junction kiosk at the beginning of the Hobbit Trail; turn right to follow the Wind in the Woods Trail.

3.2 Come to a trail junction; turn right to rejoin the trail through Greenlees Grove.

3.4 Come to a trail junction; turn right to follow the historic Naches Trail.

3.9 Return to the first interpretive kiosk and turn right and then take an immediate left to follow the East Trail.

4.4 At a trail junction turn right to return to the kiosk and the interpretive center.

4.5 Arrive at the interpretive center and the trailhead.

18 Glacier View Wilderness Area: Puyallup Trail #248 to Goat Lake

This hike has it all: a challenging yet relatively easy trail through a pristine and isolated wilderness with meadows, mountains, and an alpine lake. The high-altitude, close-up view of Mt. Rainier alone is worth the drive up the primitive road to the trailhead. The trail does not require climbing, scrambling, or any dangerous maneuvers; nonetheless, you'll be glad you're prepared with trekking poles, boots with good treads, and plenty of water.

Distance: 5.0 miles out and back
Approximate hiking time: 4 hours
Difficulty: More challenging
Trail surface: Dirt
Best season: Late June to early October; snow may still be on sections of the trail in early summer
Other trail users: Equestrians
Canine compatibility: Leashed dogs permitted
Fees and permits: No fees or permits required; fill out a free registration form at the trailhead kiosk and keep a copy with you on the trail.
Schedule: Open daily, 24 hours a day, from late June to early October; contact the US Forest Service for road and trail conditions.
Maps: USGS Mount Wow, WA; Washington State map
Trail contacts: US Forest Service; (360) 497-1100; 11024 US Highway 12, Randle; www.fs .fed.us/gpnf

Finding the trailhead: The trailhead is approximately one hour from Tacoma. From I-5, take exit 127 (WA 512). Take the WA 161 exit off WA 512 and drive south on WA 161 until it ends at WA 7. Turn left onto WA 7. At Elbe, the road divides: WA 7 turns off to the

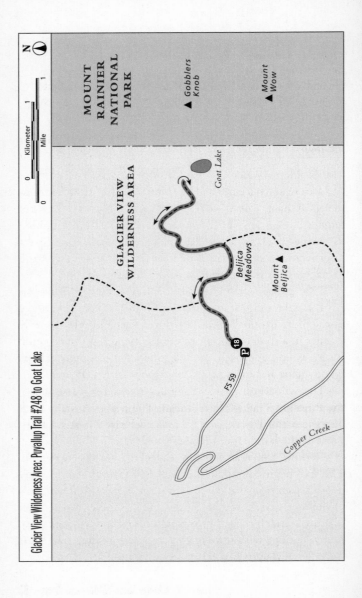

Glacier View Wilderness Area: Puyallup Trail #248 to Goat Lake

N

MOUNT
RAINIER
NATIONAL
PARK

▲ Gobblers Knob

▲ Mount Wow

GLACIER VIEW WILDERNESS AREA

Goat Lake

Beljica Meadows

▲ Mount Beljica

18 P

FS 59

Copper Creek

0   Kilometer   1
0   Mile   1

right and WA 706 begins straight ahead. Take WA 706 toward Mount Rainier National Park. Three miles past Ashford, turn left onto FS 59. (The road and sign are hard to spot—if you enter the national park, you have driven too far.) FS 59 is a primitive dirt road that climbs roughly 2,800 feet in 8 miles; a parking area and signed trailhead are near the end of the road. GPS: N46 47.38' / W121 57.10'

The Hike

The Wilderness Act of 1964 describes a wilderness area as "an area where the earth and its community of life are untrammeled by man, where man himself is a visitor who does not remain . . . an area of undeveloped Federal land retaining its primeval character and influence, without permanent improvements or human habitation, which is protected and managed so as to preserve its natural conditions . . ."

This passage aptly describes Glacier View Wilderness Area, a wild and primeval part of Gifford Pinchot National Forest. The Mount Rainier National Park boundary is only 2 miles in a straight line from the trailhead and the drive up FS 59 as you approach the trail offers jaw-dropping close-range views and unsurpassed photo ops of Mt. Rainier.

The wilderness area actually begins a short distance past the Puyallup Trail #248 trailhead. The trail eventually leads into the national park, but the route described here ends just short of the park's boundary at Goat Lake.

Getting to Goat Lake is easy—it's mostly downhill. The trail begins at an altitude of 4,650 feet and surprisingly doesn't pack the wallop of elevation gain typical on most of the area's trails. Instead, it descends 300 feet to the lake. Its initial stretch meanders through forest and an open area, follows a ridge with stunning views across a valley, and skirts the edge of Beljica Meadows, alive with blooms in midsummer. The trail continues through a deep forest and finally reaches Goat Lake, which rests in a basin beneath forested mountains. After a rest, turn around and begin the ascent back up the trail to the trailhead.

Besides carrying the essentials described in the Introduction, three cautionary steps will make your visit to this wilderness more enjoyable. Before you set out on the hike, contact the US Forest Service to check on road and trail conditions; even if the road is clear, you could run into deep snow fields on the trail, cutting your hike short. Insects at high altitudes in the Cascades can be fierce in the summer, so bring insect repellent. And last, while an encounter with large wildlife, such as a bear or cougar, is extremely unlikely, this wilderness is their home; familiarize yourself with how to handle such an encounter, referenced in the "Wildlife" section of the Introduction.

Miles and Directions

0.0 The trail begins at the parking area and signed trailhead for Trail 248. Read the Wilderness Area Regulations and register at the kiosk.

0.5 At the trail junction, take the right fork. You will soon pass through conifer forest and Beljica Meadows.

1.2 At the trail junction, take the left fork.

2.5 Arrive at Goat Lake; turn around and retrace your steps.

5.0 Arrive back at the trailhead.

Clubs and Trail Groups

Several environmental, conservation, and hiking resource groups are available in the Tacoma area, ranging from clubs where members and participants can enjoy group outings to organizations that are happy to provide information about local trails.

Tacoma Mountaineers
The Tacoma branch of the organization offering trips, classes, and events related to the outdoors.
2302 North 30th St.
Tacoma, WA 98403
(253) 566-6965
www.tacomamountaineers.org

Sierra Club Cascade Chapter
Sierra Club's local chapter offers organized outings and more.
180 Nickerson St., Suite 202
Seattle, WA 98109
(206) 378-0114
www.cascade.sierraclub.org

Washington Trails Association
The group provides information about the state's trails.
2019 Third Ave., Suite 100
Seattle, WA 98121
(206) 625-1367
www.wta.org

About the Author

Allen Cox, a third-generation Northwesterner, was born and raised in Tacoma and has been appreciating the outdoors on foot since he was old enough to walk. Sharing his love for his home turf and beyond through his writing seemed the next logical step. Allen's writing about travel, the outdoors, food and wine, and the arts has appeared in regional, national, and international publications. He has a special interest in green travel, soft-adventure travel, recreation, conservation, and geotourism. When Allen is not traveling or writing for magazines and guidebooks, he works as a communications consultant, commercial copywriter, and editor.